...st established
...known travel brands,
the experts in travel.

For more than 135 years our
guidebooks have unlocked the secrets
of destinations around the world,
sharing with travellers a wealth of
experience and a passion for travel.

**Rely on Thomas Cook as your
travelling companion on your next trip
and benefit from our uni... ...nge.**

...Cook **pocket** guides

CAMBRIDGE

Thomas
Cook

Your travelling companion since 1873

Written by James Stewart

Published by Thomas Cook Publishing
A division of Thomas Cook Tour Operations Limited
Company registration no. 3772199 England
The Thomas Cook Business Park, Unit 9, Coningsby Road
Peterborough PE3 8SB, United Kingdom
Email: books@thomascook.com, Tel: +44 (0)1733 416477
www.thomascookpublishing.com

Produced by Cambridge Publishing Management Limited
Burr Elm Court, Main Street, Caldecote CB23 7NU
www.cambridgepm.co.uk

ISBN: 978-1-84848-461-0

This first edition © 2010 Thomas Cook Publishing
Text © Thomas Cook Publishing
Cartography supplied by Redmoor Design, Tavistock, Devon
Map data © OpenStreetMap contributors CC-BY-SA, www.openstreetmap.org,
www.creativecommons.org

Series Editor: Karen Beaulah
Production/DTP: Steven Collins

Printed and bound in Spain by GraphyCems

Cover photography © Thomas Cook Publishing

CONTENTS

SYMBOLS KEY

The following symbols are used throughout this book:

ⓐ address ☎ telephone ⓦ website address
🕐 opening times 🚇 public transport connections ❶ important

The following symbols are used on the maps:

ℹ️	information office	🟦	POI (point of interest)
✈️	airport	○	city
🛡️	police station	○	small town
🚌	bus station	○	village
🚆	railway station	=	motorway
✝	cathedral or church	—	main road
P�e	park & ride	—	minor road
🛍️	shopping	—	railway
✉️	post office		
❶	numbers denote featured cafés, restaurants & venues		

PRICE CATEGORIES

The ratings below indicate average price rates for a double room per night, including breakfast:
£ under £99 ££ £100–199 £££ over £200
The typical cost for a three-course meal without drinks, is as follows:
£ under £15 ££ £16–39 £££ over £40

▶ *King's College chapel towers above the town centre*

 INTRODUCING
Cambridge

Introduction

It is acclaimed worldwide for academic excellence and the 31 colleges that make up its university have produced a quota of figureheads in the sciences, arts, philosophy and politics out of all proportion to its size. Yet, for all its erudition, Cambridge is a city that appeals to the heart as much as the head. Smaller and more charming than its great rival Oxford – known as 'the other place' in academic circles – it is a town of strong images: of soaring Gothic chapels and hushed Tudor courtyards; narrow medieval streets that are a blur with bicycles; gowned choirs in candlelit chapels at Christmas; leafy parks where students laze around on sunny days; and, of course, it is a town of punts on the willow-fringed River Cam. Small wonder 4.6 million people visit every year.

A beautiful streetscape and centuries-old academic institutions ensure that Cambridge is a place where history and tradition are an integral part of the scenery. Strolling around colleges like Trinity, where porters wear bowler hats and an 18th-century wing is modern, feels like stepping into another era.

But Cambridge is no museum piece. The presence of thousands of students having the time of their lives brings vibrancy to its timeless looks, and the foresight of town planners to ban traffic from parts of the centre promotes a lively street life. The compact historic core is invariably abuzz with shoppers, buskers, students and visitors soaking up the atmosphere. Add in the fact that parks and meadows reach right into the centre and you have a destination tailor-made for relaxed exploration, especially in spring and summer, when Cambridge's atmosphere is at its best.

The joy of modern Cambridge is that while its historic university remains central to everyday life, academic tradition is worn lightly. You can take in architecture while high-street shopping or peruse world-class antiquities and art, then walk for just ten minutes to idly sip a pint in the sunshine by the river. Cambridge is a city that is as convivial as it is cultured – the best sort of city there is.

⬤ *Expect to see bicycles everywhere you go*

When to go

SEASONS & CLIMATE

Cambridgeshire is in the driest region of Britain; average daytime temperatures are 3°C (37°F) in January and 22°C (72°F) in July. Rain is possible at any time of the year, though, so come prepared.

The town is at its best in warmer months and at its liveliest during the post-exam festivities of June, when the 'May Bumps' and college balls take place. If the weather smiles, midsummer (July–August) is quintessential Cambridge: all punting on the Cam, picnics in meadows and lazy pints outside pubs. However, the town is incredibly popular at this time of year. Accommodation is often at a premium, so advance booking is essential.

Late summer and early autumn can be lovely, the students return after the summer break, the town is calmer and looks splendid under crisp, clear skies, while in December there are magical Christmas concerts in historic buildings.

● *In spring the Backs are speckled with wild flowers*

ANNUAL EVENTS

May

Cambridge Beer Festival Hundreds of real ales, ciders, English wines and meads are celebrated in the longest-running booze-up in the country, attracting around 32,000 visitors over the last week in the month. ⓦ www.cambridgebeerfestival.com

June

College balls Entry is restricted to students but the fireworks displays can be admired from afar.

May Bumps Boat crews race down the Cam beside Midsummer Common during the intercollegiate races, held over four days in mid-June. ⓦ www.cucbc.org/bumps

Midsummer Fair The end of the month sees the arrival of craft stalls and a funfair for this fair on Midsummer Common, a tradition since medieval times. ⓦ www.cambridge.gov.uk

July

Cambridge Folk Festival One of the world's longest-running music festivals, a fixture since the mid-1960s, the Folk Festival brings an eclectic mix of international, traditional and contemporary folk, blues and rock acts to the suburb of Cherry Hinton. Highly recommended.
ⓦ www.cambridgefolkfestival.co.uk

September

Cambridge Film Festival This excellent festival based at the Arts Picturehouse has a track record of breaking cult releases in the UK. ⓦ www.cambridgefilmfestival.org.uk

History

Cambridge made its debut as a tribal settlement beside a ford on the Granta river, near today's Magdalene Bridge. The Romans recognised the location's strategic importance as a staging post on the Colchester–Chester road and stationed troops here – first to protect the ford in 43 AD, then to fight off Boudicca's Iceni tribe in 50 AD. Although the Roman settlement grew into a town, it took Mercian King Offa to build a bridge over the river. Apart from a hiccup during Viking raids, 'Grantebridge' was a thriving settlement when Norman troops marched into town after 1066. Like the Romans, they suffered raids – this time from

⬥ *This statue of Henry VIII looks down onto King's Parade*

Saxon Hereward the Wake, whose rebel base was in marshland near Ely – and promptly built a castle for security. Its motte remains uphill from the bridge.

What changed the backwater's destiny was the arrival of scholars from Oxford in 1209; they were evicted, the story goes, for riots against Oxford residents. More students followed, so in 1284 the Bishop of Ely founded a college modelled upon the monastic community, today's Peterhouse. As in Oxford, tension between town and gown flared into violence during a peasants' rebellion in 1381. Unlike in Oxford, legal and religious authorities sided with the scholars – academia now held sway in Cambridge.

Other powerful patrons followed suit, then so did royal patrons such as Henry IV, who established King's College, and Trinity College's founder, Henry VIII. It's ironic, then, that a former Sidney Sussex student briefly ended the monarchy – Oliver Cromwell.

Normal service was resumed with the restoration of Charles II to the throne. Colleges flourished again to produce a Who's Who of artistic, scientific and philosophical minds, British and foreign alike. All were men until the 1870s, when the university accepted women for the first time – it would take another 70 years before they were awarded degrees too. The Victorian town, meanwhile, was wrestling with the rapid expansion brought about by the railway, and suburbs began to circle the historic core. Expansion continued into the 1980s, when Cambridge's university helped to fund a science park in Fenland two miles north of the town, a hugely profitable venture that became known as 'Silicon Fen', after California's 'Silicon Valley'.

Culture

Marlowe and Monty Python, Plath and Pink Floyd... Cambridge has produced more than its share of culture. During term time you can expect a vibrant repertoire of classical concerts from the myriad college ensembles and choirs, generally at low prices and regularly in outstanding settings. The Cambridge Corn Exchange (see page 70) also runs a wide-ranging programme of music, dance and other shows.

The Cambridge Arts Theatre (see page 70) attracts high-quality productions, with many shows that come directly from or prior to the London West End. In July and August is the city's Shakespeare Festival, during which the bard's plays are performed in college gardens. For comedy fans, the Cambridge Footlights student revue is always worth checking out.

The town also has a good spread of museums. The Fitzwilliam Museum (see pages 64–6) is superb, while exhibitions at Kettle's Yard (see pages 56–7) are worth investigating.

CHRISTMAS AT KING'S

No event in Cambridge's cultural calendar is more celebrated than the Christmas Eve carol service in King's College chapel. The concert is held at 15.00 and tickets are available on the day from 07.30 – queue early to secure a ticket. The King's choir also sings Evensong daily during term time. ⓦ www.kings.cam.ac.uk/choir

❯ *You might see members of the university in ceremonial garb*

 # MAKING THE MOST OF
Cambridge

Shopping

Prosperous and professional, Cambridge allows for a good session of retail therapy. A surprising number of designer names have a presence in the town despite its modest size and, although the chain stores have most definitely commandeered prime retail space in the town centre, plenty of smaller independent outlets and markets remain, offering individual wares. And, of course, there are all the university outlets that sell striped college scarves and sweatshirts – the classic Cambridge souvenir.

There's no better introduction to Cambridge than the daily market on **Market Hill**, whose stalls are Cambridge in microcosm: there are second-hand threads, books and records for students; artisan breads and cheeses for the town's well-heeled professionals; crafts stalls and souvenirs for tourists; as well as the usual clothing and fruit and veg. A crafts and farmers' market takes over on Sunday, while a smaller crafts and art market is held in **All Saints Garden**, opposite Trinity College, on Saturdays.

The core of the shopping centre spans the streets east of Market Hill: **Petty Cury**, a fairly bland pedestrian street occupied by high-street chains, and malls Lion Yard and Grand Arcade, the latter the town's most recent development occupied by prestige brands, including a five-storey John Lewis department store; and **Sidney Street**, which has more major names.

The quintessential Cambridge shopping streets, however, are **King's Parade** and **Trinity Street** on the other side of the market. Fronted by colleges and ornate shop fronts, this historic strip represents a must-browse for visitors. The former has women's clothing, galleries and crafts boutiques, plus traditional college outfitter Ryder & Amies, while pretty cobbled Trinity Street offers an engaging mix of high-street names like Reiss, Jigsaw and Jaeger, independent fashion outlets and a couple of excellent bookshops, including that of Cambridge University Press. Narrow **Rose Crescent** and **Green Street** off Trinity Street are worth a detour for interesting smaller shops; the former has a couple of fine jewellers.

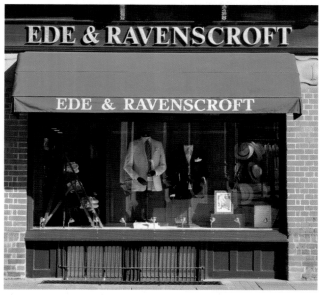

○ *Traditional English tailors and robemakers thrive in Cambridge*

Eating & drinking

Blame impoverished students and a resident population that lives in surrounding neighbourhoods. How else can you explain the apparent preference for casual fare over fine dining in central Cambridge? In the centre, **King's Parade**, **Bene't Street** and **Trinity Street** host a selection of informal cafés and bistros,

⬤ *Enjoy a riverside seat at The Anchor*

and stalls at the market will rustle up noodles, soups and jacket spuds for lunch on the go. Bridge Street is another area to browse, with outlets of restaurant chains such as Ask and Côte, the Italian and French bistros. These are reliable if not particularly exciting.

Notwithstanding the central options listed in this guide, head outside the centre for fine dining – Michelin-rated **Midsummer House** (see pages 75–6) on Midsummer Common is 15 minutes' walk from Bridge Street and the **Oak Bistro** (see page 75) near Parker's Piece is the same distance from the colleges and museums around Downing Street. Picnickers, however, are spoiled for choice: pick up the ingredients in the market then head to Jesus Green, Midsummer Common, Coe Fen or Sheep's Green to picnic beside the river. Better still, hire a punt and head upriver to eat in the meadows around Grantchester as students have for a century or so.

Students may not be the world's greatest gourmets but they have always liked a drink, and a town that has hosted student boozers like Pepys and Byron boasts some excellent pubs. Generally, pubs come in two varieties in Cambridge: historic establishments of creaky floorboards and old wood like **The Eagle** (touristy but essential; see page 71) and **The Pickerel** (see page 59), and those in appealing locations, like **The Anchor** (see page 59) or **The Granta** (see page 78) sited beside the River Cam. All these are Cambridge classics, so liable to suffer from crowds. In high season – or just to sample locals' Cambridge – it's worth walking to pubs out of the town centre: the **Free Press** (see page 77) off Parker's Piece is a delight and drinkers can lose a happy evening bouncing between pubs off Mill Road.

Entertainment

The surprise of Cambridge is that a vivacious university life does not necessarily translate into a huge variety of options for a night out. Most college events are for students only and, without some research, Cambridge can appear to be every inch the pleasant provincial town it is despite its heavyweight reputation. Local newspaper the *Cambridge Evening News* contains listings of weekly entertainment, or source venue flyers in the visitor information centre.

That said, there's always something going on throughout the week – especially during term time – and anyone with a penchant for pub culture will find the town a pleasure to explore. With plenty of historic pubs and bars to choose from, you're unlikely to run out of venues, even though there is no central bar or nightlife district for bar-hopping and your options in terms of modern style bars are more limited. A couple of options by Magdalene Bridge are worth considering in summer.

A few pubs also host rock gigs, notably the Portland Arms at 129 Chesterton Road, which plays host to bands on most nights. However, professional rock acts – including major international names – are served by the town's two principal venues, the **Cambridge Corn Exchange** (see page 70) and **The Junction** (see page 78). These also host theatre, although the main stages are the two theatres in the city centre, the **Cambridge Arts Theatre** (see page 70) and **ADC Theatre** (☎ 01223 300085 ⓦ www.adctheatre.com); the latter on Park Street hosts the student Footlights Revue in June, the launch pad for a roll call of British comedic talent. Notwithstanding venues such as **Fez** (see page 71) in the centre, which hosts clubs every night in term time, or The Junction, clubbing in Cambridge is fairly provincial – most venues only open Thur–Sat and cater to a boozy post-pub crowd.

Finally, a special mention should go to two Cambridge festivals: the Beer Festival in May is the country's largest event outside London – 32,000 drinkers in a week can't all be wrong – while the town's July folk festival is arguably the best of its kind in Britain.

⬤ The Junction – a hub for music, dance, theatre and comedy

Sport & relaxation

SPECTATOR SPORTS
Football
Modern football was born here – rules were drawn up by two students in 1848 and trialled on Parker's Piece – but Cambridge has never been an ardent supporter. The town's main team is **Cambridge United**, lodged in the Conference League since relegation from the Football League in 2005. They are based at the Abbey Stadium on Newmarket Road (◉ Bus: Citi 3). Tickets cost around £12–18 depending on the stand and can be bought at the gate.

Rugby & rowing
The eastern counties' most successful rugby club, Cambridge Rugby Club's first XV play in National League 1. Tickets are available at the gate of Wests Renault Park on Grantchester Road, south-east of the centre, for around £10. Arguably the

> **TIPS FROM A PUNTING PRO**
> 'First-timers should remember Newton's law of motion: each action must have an equal and opposite reaction. There's no need to use brute force; instead, plant your feet and use your body weight not your arms, then steer by trailing the pole in the water as a rudder. Try to stay on the right-hand side of the river. If a collision is unavoidable, it's the done thing to warn occupants of the other punt.'

biggest date in the calendar is the university Varsity Match against students of Oxford – a grudge match since 1872. It is traditionally held in December, usually in Twickenham, London. Cambridge University is famously more passionate still about its rowing. As well as the famous Boat Race on the Thames at the end of March, intercollegiate rowing races are held on the Cam in early June.

PARTICIPATION SPORTS

No visit is complete without messing about in a punt. Rental is available at Magadalene Bridge, at the bridge behind Trinity College and at Silver Street Bridge, beside Queens' College; the latter is the start for the trip to Grantchester. Punts come in two sizes (up to 6 or 12 people) and cost around £15–18 per hour, usually with a minimum charge and a hefty deposit on a credit card. Although it's most fun to try your hand (see box opposite) – even when the Cam is carnage in late July and August – chauffeured punt tours are also available. Assuming you don't accidentally do it while punting, you can swim at Parkside Pools (Gonville Place) and in summer in a lido at Jesus Green.

● *No trip to Cambridge would be complete without a punting trip*

Accommodation

There is a wealth of hotels and guesthouses available in Cambridge. During the high season, the high number of visitors to Cambridge does mean that booking your reservation well in advance is highly recommended, and it's worth noting that finding cheap accommodation can be difficult. However, cheaper guesthouses and B&Bs can be found around 20 minutes' walk from the pedestrian core. Alternatively, those with an academic bent might want to look into one of the colleges' B&Bs. From 2010, colleges such as Corpus Christi, Christ's, Jesus and Emmanuel will take guests during college holidays; prices start at £35 per person. Visit ⓦ www.conferencecambridge.com for information and reservations. The nearest campsite is three miles from the centre in Great Shelford village.

HOTELS & GUESTHOUSES

Ashley Hotel £ It may be fairly old-fashioned but this traditional comfy B&B represents good value considering the location: a 15-minute walk from the centre via Jesus Green. Note that check-in between 14.00–17.00 is in more expensive sister hotel Arundel House, a few hundred metres away on the same road. ⓐ 74–76 Chesterton Road ⓣ 01223 350059 ⓦ www.arundelhousehotels.co.uk

Cityroomz £ This former warehouse outside the train station now hosts hostel-style accommodation. There's not a great deal of space in the cabin-like rooms, which come with bunkbeds or

doubles with futon mattresses, but they are clean and cheap.
ⓐ Station Road ⓣ 01223 304050 ⓦ www.cityroomz.com

Springfield House £ Ten miles from the centre, yet good road links and an excellent bus service make this lovely villa a retreat par excellence from Cambridge's summer crowds. The garden is a delight and pubs in the village serve dinner. ⓐ 14–16 Horn Lane, Linton ⓣ 01223 891383 ⓦ www.springfieldhouse.org

Warkworth House £ A good location in a side road by Parker's Piece and excellent cooked breakfasts are the appeal at Warkworth House, the largest guesthouse in the centre. Rooms, all of which are en suite, are spacious and homely in pastel shades. Superiors are worth an extra £10 for the additional space. ⓐ Warkworth Terrace ⓣ 01223 363682 ⓦ www.warkworthhouse.co.uk

Crowne Plaza ££ A typically slick and efficient outpost of the international Crowne chain, with 198 modern rooms and an appealingly central location that puts you within a five-minute walk of both the colleges and shops. ⓐ Downing Street ⓣ 0870 400 9180 ⓦ www.crowneplaza.com/cambridgeuk

Regent Hotel ££ Pleasant modern en-suite rooms in the blonde wood and stainless steel vein in a small hotel in a Georgian house, centrally located on Parker's Piece. Standard rooms are small but are well-priced for the location. Executive rooms come with park views.ⓐ 41 Regent Street ⓣ 01223 351470 ⓦ www.regenthotel.co.uk

Royal Cambridge ££ Fronted by a former Georgian terrace, this cosy hotel is full of the faded elegance of a bygone era. Only a ten-minute walk from King's Parade, the Royal also boasts on-site parking for only a fiver. ⓐ Trumpington Street (junction with Lensfield Road) ⓣ 01223 351631 ⓦ www.theroyalcambridgehotel.co.uk

University Arms ££ The Beatles had to be smuggled out in the head porter's car and John Cleese worked in the bar as a student. This imposing Victorian pile remains a local institution. It's good value for the central location, though, and there's a bar overlooking Parker's Piece. ⓐ Regent Street ⓣ 01223 273000 ⓦ www.devere.co.uk

Doubletree by Hilton £££ There can be no faulting the location of this Hilton-affiliated hotel: moments from Queens' College and with views of punts beyond the window. Renovation has introduced modern style to create an international-standard hotel. Deluxe rooms and suites have the river views, all standards have Wi-Fi and there's a large heated pool. ⓐ Granta Place, Mill Lane ⓣ 01223 259988 ⓦ www.doubletreebyhilton.co.uk/cambridge

Hotel du Vin £££ Four houses were knocked through to create this location of the boutique chain, which features contemporary glamour and individually decorated rooms. Well located near the Fitzwilliam Museum, yet with quiet back rooms. ⓐ 15–19 Trumpington Street ⓣ 01223 227330 ⓦ www.hotelduvin.com

Hotel Felix £££ It's a mile north of the centre, but for that you get a very Cambridge interpretation of a boutique hotel – a Victorian villa in spacious gardens whose generous and stylish bedrooms prioritise comfort above sleek looks. The understated chic extends to the excellent restaurant, Graffiti.
ⓐ Whitehouse Lane, Huntingdon Road ⓣ 01223 277977
ⓦ www.hotelfelix.co.uk

HOSTELS & CAMPING

Cambridge Camping and Caravanning Club £ The closest campsite to the centre offers ample facilities for the caravans of its older clientele and its neat field also has space for tents. It's in a village 5 km (3 miles) from the centre and linked by bus 7. ⓐ 19 Cabbage Moor ⓣ 01223 841185
ⓦ www.campingandcaravanningclub.co.uk ⓛ End Mar–Oct

Cambridge YHA £ The cheapest beds in Cambridge are in this friendly association hostel installed in a Victorian house near the station; all but ten double rooms are dormitories. Facilities include a self-catering kitchen (cooked meals are also available) and laundry. Very popular with groups in summer.
ⓐ 97 Tenison Road ⓣ 0845 371 9728 ⓦ www.yha.org.uk

THE BEST OF CAMBRIDGE

The university dominates life in Cambridge and no visit is complete without a visit to a couple of colleges. However, anyone with a penchant for lazy hedonism will find the town a joy, especially in summer.

TOP 10 ATTRACTIONS

- **Walk along the Backs** From the chapel of King's to punts under Clare College bridge and the Bridge of Sighs – this pleasant 1-km (½-mile) stroll along the riverside back gardens of the colleges takes you past some of the town's most iconic sights (see page 44).

- **King's College Chapel** Not just the highlight of collegiate Cambridge, but one of the pinnacles of Gothic architecture in Europe (see pages 47–8).

- **Trinity College** The grandest college in appearance is a postcard-perfect vision of old world academia – the ideal setting for some of the most famous student stories in Cambridge (see pages 53–5).

- **Kettle's Yard** Is it a museum? Is it a gallery? Actually it's a bit of both – an enchanting gallery that puts 20th-century British art in a stylish domestic setting, as well as showing interesting exhibitions in a modern display space (see pages 56–7).

- **Fitzwilliam Museum** The blockbuster hoard of antiquities and world ceramics, sculpture and painting in one of Britain's oldest public museums would do credit to a capital city. Make sure to tie your shoelaces unlike one hapless visitor in 2006... (see pages 64–6).

- **Punting** Messing about on the River Cam is a must-do experience – tour along the Backs for classic Cambridge, head upriver to Grantchester for a gentle escape or go chauffeur-driven if you're nervous (see page 20).

- **Pubs** With historic inns like The Eagle (see page 71), and gems such as the Free Press (see page 77), Cambridge is proof that culture can come in pint glasses.

- **Market** Browse stalls of the marvellous daily market to get a taste of Cambridge.

- **Cambridge Folk Festival** Running for over 40 years, and one of the oldest music festivals in the world, this continues to attract major international names in rock and folk for its four-day jamboree (see page 9).

- **Picnicking** Whether on Jesus Green or Midsummer Common, by millponds or on the meadows around Grantchester, a lazy lunch alfresco is one of the delights of summer in Cambridge.

◗ *A picturesque passage leads to Jesus College*

Suggested itineraries

Your at-a-glance guide to all the best that Cambridge has to offer, programmed around how much time you have.

HALF-DAY: CAMBRIDGE IN A HURRY

If you're only in Cambridge for a business trip or flying visit, restrict yourself to the college quarter to do justice to the historic core. Begin at Queens' College (see pages 50–51) for a journey back to the Tudor origins of the college establishments, then head to King's College (see pages 47–8) for its outstanding chapel and stock up on college clobber in Ryder & Amies (see page 58). Continue up Trinity Street to see the splendid Great Court of Trinity College (see pages 53–5) and the Wren Library (see page 55), then continue to St John's to see the Bridge of Sighs (see page 52) and cut through to return along the Backs.

1 DAY: TIME TO SEE A LITTLE MORE

With more time, follow the half-day agenda to St John's College, then stop in the Norman Round Church (see page 51). Now head up Bridge Street to tour the unique and arty house of Kettle's Yard (see pages 56–7), then pick up a punt at Magdalene Bridge to tour the Backs on the River Cam. Alternatively, continue your college tour after the church by visiting Jesus College (see pages 61–2), then taking a break for shopping in Sidney Street, the Grand Arcade and the splendid market. Fortified by a late lunch, head south via Pembroke and Peterhouse colleges to the Fitzwilliam Museum on Trumpington Street (see pages 64–6) – allow two hours at least to tour its collections.

2–3 DAYS OR MORE: TIME TO SEE MUCH MORE

Extra time affords you a chance to really get under the skin of
Cambridge and see beyond the main sights. So, as well as the
must-see colleges and the 'Fitz' museum, you should take a walk
along Jesus Green and Midsummer Common, stop in lesser-
known (and free) colleges such as Christ's and Emmanuel as a
breather from shopping in the town centre. You should also
investigate pubs such as the Cambridge Blue (see page 77) or
riverside Granta (see page 78). Don't miss trips out of
Cambridge to Grantchester (see page 80) – better still set aside
a half-day to visit on foot or by punt – or out to Ely (see page 84)
for the cathedral or, with your own transport, to Wicken Fen (see
page 86).

● *The town centre is chock-a-block with college buildings*

Something for nothing

With history everywhere you look, Cambridge is not an expensive town to enjoy; just strolling streets like **King's Parade** and **Trinity Street** is a pleasure, especially when buskers set up in summer, and the market is ideal for a browse – **Grand Arcade** nearby is slicker and more expensive. Many sights are also free, notably the **colleges**. Along the River Cam, Corpus Christi, Gonville & Caius and Magdalene do not levy an entrance charge to visitors, nor do any of the colleges away from the river, so you can admire chapels by Sir Christopher Wren (Pembroke and Emmanuel Colleges) without paying a penny.

All but one of the museums are free too. Those of a scientific or naturalistic bent will find much to enjoy; the **Fitzwilliam Museum** (see pages 64–6) is an essential stop for any cultured visitor; and mementoes of polar heroes make the **Scott Polar Research Institute and Museum** (see page 75) surprisingly moving. Much of the town's appeal lies in its green spaces, which were preserved by Victorian planners during the rapid expansion of the 1800s. Take your time along the **Backs** (a tip: continue across Silver Street to the river meadows south) or stroll in parks such as Jesus Green and Midsummer Common.

When it rains

Thankfully, prevailing weather patterns mean rain-sodden days are not common, yet nor are they unknown. While much of Cambridge's appeal is outdoors on the streets and in college courts, some sights seem well-suited for downpours. You can easily lose an hour examining the detail of **King's College Chapel** (see pages 47–8) – time it right during term and you could stay for an Evensong concert – or explore gems such as **Pepys Library** in Magdalene College (see pages 48–9). And, of course, there are the museums: scuttle along Downing Street between showers to see university displays of zoology, geology, anthropology and archaeology. The **Fitzwilliam Museum** (see pages 64–6) around the corner from these is perfect for wet days, with an eclectic hoard of antiquities, applied arts and painting. If you fancy a bit of retail therapy, both the **Grand Arcade** and the **Grafton Centre** are under cover.

You could also head out of town to Europe's finest air museum at **Duxford** (see pages 80 & 82) or to **Ely** (see pages 84–5), with its cathedral and teashops. And if all else fails, there are few finer ways to pass a dreary afternoon than to hunker down in a historic Cambridge pub – you're spoiled for choice.

On arrival

ARRIVING

Good road and rail connections, plus proximity to Stansted
airport, mean that you have a number of options for getting to
Cambridge. The main routes for driving to Cambridge are the
M11 motorway, providing access to the south and west of the
city, and the A14, which brings you around the north and east.
Both roads are convenient for getting to the city's Park & Ride
schemes, which provide free parking in outlying locations and
frequent and fast bus services into the heart of the city (see
'Getting around').

This is well worth considering on a day trip since the traffic
in the city can be heavy and parking in the centre and
surrounding neighbourhoods can be tricky. With pedestrian
zones and rising bollards to contend with, the centre is best
avoided in a car. A higher than average number of cyclists might
also take some drivers by surprise – check your blind spots, try to
give them room and don't be disconcerted if you find them
coming towards you on one-way streets and weaving between
the rush hour traffic.

One of the fastest ways to get to Cambridge from central
London is by rail: there are regular services from King's Cross
(convenient also for international passengers arriving at London
St Pancras) and Liverpool Street. Cambridge also enjoys
excellent connections from Scotland and the North via
Peterborough, as well as regional services from Birmingham and
the Midlands, East Anglia and the north-west. The train station
lies just over a mile south of the centre; allow 20–25 minutes to

walk into town. Buses 1, 3 or 7 offer a fast and frequent service to the central terminus; see 'Getting around' for details of tickets. A taxi to the town centre will cost around £5.

Those travelling from further afield might choose to fly to Stansted, lying a convenient 42 km (30 miles) south of Cambridge, and then catch a train or coach into the city. The hourly trains take 33 minutes, while **National Express** coaches 797, 787 and 717 depart approximately hourly for the 55-minute journey to the coach terminal at Parkside, beside Parker's Piece.

National Express coaches also link Cambridge to Gatwick and Heathrow airports and cities throughout the UK. Budget coach carrier **Megabus** connects to Oxford, with single fares from as low as £1. Its terminus is also at Parkside.

FINDING YOUR FEET

The town centre is largely pedestrianised, although be aware that small town buses traverse some streets such as Trinity Street. Foreign visitors should be aware that traffic comes from the right (not the left) in the UK. More problematic are Cambridge's cyclists, which leave streets a blur of bicycles. In theory, they also come from the right and at modest speed. In practice, look both ways twice when crossing the road.

ORIENTATION

Though Cambridge is a small town and easy to navigate, a map is always useful; as well as the one provided in this book, maps can be bought (50p) from the Visitor Information Centre (see page 93) and from a dispenser (£1) directly outside the train station. For tourists, the main area of interests are those demarcated by this

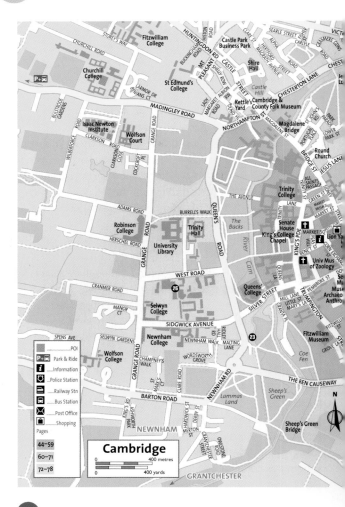

Cambridge

	POI
P+🚗	Park & Ride
ℹ️	Information
🚓	Police Station
🚆	Railway Stn
🚌	Bus Station
✉️	Post Office
🛍️	Shopping

Pages

44–59
60–71
72–78

0   400 metres
0   400 yards

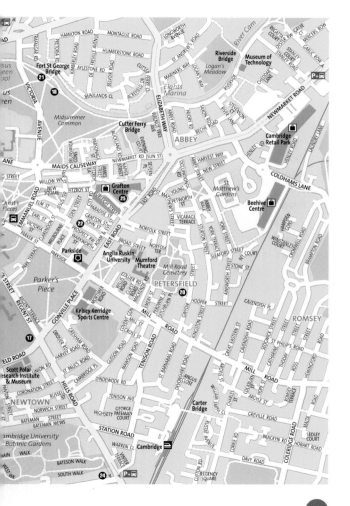

book: the college quarter west of King's Parade and Trinity Street to the River Cam for the most historic colleges and punting; the commercial centre, roughly the area wedged between King's Parade/Trinity Street and Sidney Street/St Andrew's Street, for the main shopping streets, some less-visited colleges and, to the south, the museums. Beyond the city centre the tourist sights are largely replaced with pleasant green spaces such as Jesus Green and a slice of everyday Cambridge on Mill Road; however, there are always exceptions to the rule such as the Scott Polar Research Museum and the Botanic Garden.

GETTING AROUND

This compact city is easy to manage on foot. With time on your side, one of the best ways to experience the centre is to explore by instinct and dive down whichever historic street looks interesting; as an idea of distances, it will only take about 10–15 minutes to walk without stops from Queens' College to the Round Church. However, for outlying sights or to reach the centre from the outskirts it is worth considering a bus.

By bus

Bus lines are operated by Stagecoach (📞 01223 423578 🌐 www.stagecoachbus.com), which prefixes route numbers by the tag 'Citi'. All operate from a terminal in the centre of the shopping area, including the Park & Ride buses that traverse from one side of Cambridge to another. Buses go approximately every 10 minutes, and the most useful tickets for tourists are the Day Rider travel pass (£3.30) and Mega Rider seven-day ticket (£11). Be aware that most routes are designed to provide transport predominantly between the centre and the suburban districts. Consequently the handiest service for visitors is the smaller green City Circle bus. This free service runs every 15 minutes 09.00–17.00 Mon–Sat (but not Sun & bank holidays) and operates a one-way circuit of Downing Street–Midsummer Common–Jesus Lane–Trinity Street/King's Parade–Pembroke Street.

Park & Ride

All sites are well signposted off major routes: the M11 provides easy access to the car parks at Trumpington (Junction 11) and Madingley Road (Junction 13); the A14 to those at Milton (Junction 33) and Newmarket Road (Junction 35). There is a fifth site on Babraham Road, south of the town near Addenbrooke's Hospital. Bus services connect each to the centre approximately every 10 minutes from 07.00–20.30 Mon–Sat and 09.00–18.00 Sun & bank holidays. Return tickets cost £2.20 from vending machines or £2.50 on the bus.

○ *Fast trains from Cambridge connect to London in under an hour*

By bike

A bicycle is by far the most convenient means of travelling from outlying neighbourhoods and covering the centre quickly, as the one in four Cambridge residents who use one to commute to work will testify. Bike park railings are fairly widespread and the terrain is almost universally flat. Bike repair shops and hire are plentiful, although you're advised to book ahead in high season. **Station Cycles** has depots at the railway station and in the centre or try **City Cycle Hire** on Newnham Road. Expect to pay a deposit of £40–50 and a rental charge of around £10 per day or £20 per week. As in any city, it is always a good idea to lock a wheel and the frame to your chosen lamp post.

Station Cycles @ Railway station ☎ 01223 307125
ⓦ www.stationcycles.co.uk, or @ Grand Arcade, Corn Exchange Street ☎ 01223 307655

PARKING IN CAMBRIDGE

Combine a centre that is largely off-limits to car drivers and permit-only restrictions in surrounding neighbourhoods – even those a 30-minute walk away – and it's no surprise there is severe pressure on car parks in the heart of Cambridge. Expect to queue for a space – especially at weekends – for the two central car parks at Grand Arcade and Park Street (behind the Round Church). Both are open 24/7. By far the best option is to travel into the centre by the Park & Ride scheme or, if staying overnight, to ensure your hotel provides parking.

⬤ Great St Mary's church sits at the heart of Cambridge's town centre

City Cycle Hire ⓐ 61 Newnham Road ⓣ 01223 365629
ⓦ www.citycyclehire.com

Taxis

The main taxi ranks are in St Andrew's Street (opposite Christ's College), Drummer Street and at Parkside. Nighttime ranks also operate from Sidney Street (outside Boots), Bridge Street and Market Square. There's also a rank outside the train station. Note that Cambridge taxis can be hailed on the street as they pass – free cars are those with an illuminated sign on their roofs. Private hire companies include:

A1 Cabco ⓣ 01223 313131
Ace Taxis ⓣ 01223 462020
CamCab ⓣ 01223 704704
Camtax ⓣ 01223 242424
Panther ⓣ 01223 715715

Car hire

Although a car is of little use in Cambridge itself, it is handy to combine out-of-town destinations into a single day out. Costs vary by company and season, but average around £35 a day. Most offices open Mon–Sat morning.

Avis ⓐ 245 Mill Road ⓣ 0870 608 6327 ⓦ www.avis.co.uk
Cambridge Car & Van Rental ⓣ 303–305 Newmarket Road
ⓣ 01223 464045 ⓦ www.cambridgecarandvanrental.co.uk
Hertz ⓐ Station Building (railway station), Station Road
ⓣ 0870 850 2651 ⓦ www.hertz.co.uk

● *The impressive gatehouse of St John's College*

THE CITY OF
Cambridge

THE CITY

Introduction

Although you can walk from one side of the centre to the other in around 20 minutes, Cambridge nevertheless splits easily into areas. From Roman garrison settlement to medieval academic centre, the town emerged on the banks of the River Cam, so it's little surprise the college quarter is stuffed with history. Defined by the Backs on one side and King's Parade/Trinity Street on the other, this area stretching to Magdalene Bridge is full of picture-postcard images. It is the Cambridge of punts on the Cam, of gorgeous college courts like Queens' and Trinity, and of the town's defining architectural statement – the sublime Gothic chapel at King's.

The commercial centre, directly east, has history of its own – on a tour you'll find the oldest building in the county and follow in the footsteps of people like Christopher Wren, John Milton and Charles Darwin. But what characterises the area situated roughly up to Sidney Street/St Andrew's Street is Cambridge's finest shopping and the excellent daily market. A string of museums, including the must-see Fitzwilliam, balances the area's appeal. Surrounding this is the area around the tree-lined inner ring road, which is roughly everything outside the town's core, including an intriguing museum, a botanic garden and two lovely parks.

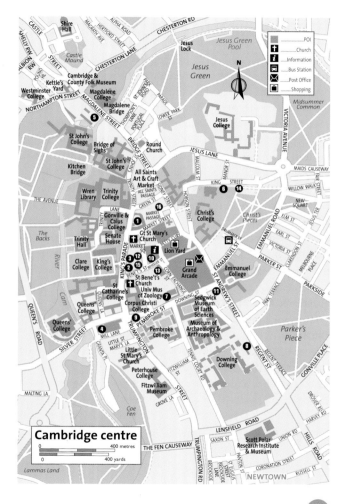

POI
Church
Information
Bus Station
Post Office
Shopping

Cambridge centre

0   400 metres
0   400 yards

The college quarter

For all the classic scenes of Cambridge, walk west of the centre. When the first colleges colonised the east bank of the River Cam river in the 13th century, they not only laid the foundations of the university, they shifted the axis of the town. Within 300 years, this area had become one of the great academic centres of Europe. Kings of England personally funded its architecture, some of which was created by the continent's finest craftsmen. In the centuries that followed, key figures in British arts and sciences spent their formative years in this 1-km (just over ½-mile) strip as students. Bounded by the Backs to the west and King's Parade and Trinity Street to the east, this historic quarter still feels removed from the everyday hubbub elsewhere. And with largely pedestrianised streets and leafy paths along the river, it is ideal for exploration on foot.

SIGHTS & ATTRACTIONS

The Backs

This park-like expanse – the back gardens of the colleges – is a lovely spot to stroll beside the Cam, especially in spring when it is ablaze with crocuses and daffodils. The walk here also takes you past some of the classic postcard scenes of Cambridge: punts under the bridge of Clare College, or King's College chapel rising behind an immaculately clipped lawn. You can make it into part of a walking loop – footbridges allow access through the colleges to Trinity Street – or take punt along the river (see page 21). **ⓐ** Queen's Road

ACCESS & ADMISSION TO CAMBRIDGE COLLEGES
Cambridge colleges remain private institutions, so their
opening times may change to suit term-time functions.
Most close to visitors during exam time, roughly from mid-
April or May to early June; call ahead for day-to-day
information. Entry costs also vary by college but as a rule
of thumb, smaller colleges and those away from the Cam
are free. Wherever you visit, staircases are out of bounds
and, unless you are a senior member of that particular
college, don't even think about setting foot on the lawn.

Clare College

The college of DNA discoverer James Watson and Sir David
Attenborough opens into a classical courtyard, completed in 1715.
It would have been sooner had Oliver Cromwell not plundered
the site for stone during the English Civil War in the 1640s. Some
Gothic features from its previous incarnation remain – Clare is the
second oldest Cambridge college, founded in 1321 – yet its most
acclaimed feature is a pretty rear footbridge over the Cam topped
by stone balls, one missing a wedge at its rear. One tale has it that
the builder removed the chunk in protest at his invoice not being
paid in full, another that a student sliced out the wedge after he
realised he had lost a bet about the number of balls – his friend
bet that there were 14, but with the slice removed there were only
13 and three-quarters. More likely is that a repair fell loose.
ⓐ Trinity Lane ☎ 01223 333200 ⓦ www.clare.cam.ac.uk
🕐 10.45–16.30 daily ⓘ £2 admission (summer)

Corpus Christi College

Another historic charmer, this is the only college in Cambridge and Oxford with civic roots. Whereas other medieval colleges were founded by royals or the religious hierarchy, 'Corpus' was established in the mid-14th century by town guilds. Such civic basis didn't shield it from town–gown tension, however, and the college found itself at the sharp end of the Peasants' Revolt in 1381. The college's gem is Old Court, Cambridge's oldest court, built in medieval times. It was already centuries old when Elizabethan playwright Christopher Marlowe bunked down there. A more enduring resident is the ghost that apparently haunts the Parker Room on M Staircase – according to one theory, it is a former undergraduate who had an affair with the Master's daughter and asphyxiated while hiding

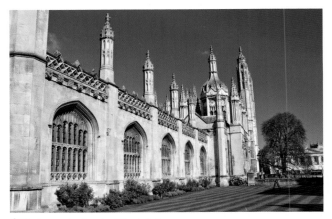

🔺 *The impressive façade of King's College*

in a cupboard. ⓐ Trumpington Street ⓣ 01223 338000
ⓦ www.corpus.cam.ac.uk ⓛ 11.00–16.00 daily (mid-June–
mid-May)

Gonville & Caius College
This small college, whose alumni include broadcaster David
Frost, is known to everyone as 'Keys' in honour of its 16th-
century co-founder John Keys – the doctor to Elizabeth I
Latinised his name to Caius after studying in Italy and returned
home to extend his old university, then plain 'Gonville'. In doing
so he gave the college its three stone gates that represented
different stages of academia: the 'Humble' porters' entrance on
Trinity Street; the 'Virtuous' gate used by students to pass
between Tree and Caius courts; and the splendid triumphal
'Honour' gate carved with classical motifs through which
graduates exit Caius Court to collect degrees in nearby Senate
House (see page 53). Keys's alabaster tomb is in the chapel.
ⓐ Trinity Street ⓣ 01223 332400 ⓦ www.gonvilleandcaius.org
ⓛ 09.00–14.00 daily

King's College
The chapel of King's is not just an icon of Cambridge but a
prized piece of Gothic architecture. A 20-year-old Henry VI
intended it as the centrepiece of a 'Great Court' when building
began in 1441 – and much of medieval Cambridge was razed to
make space. But his murder in the Tower of London, then the
diversion of funds for the Wars of the Roses, stalled the work
until the Tudors took up the baton. You can trace its history
inside. Henry's choir is pure Gothic simplicity. By the time the

builders had reached the ante-chapel 80 years later, every portal and arch was festooned with portcullises, roses and greyhounds of the victorious Tudors. More impressive still is the kaleidoscope of fan vaulting in the ceiling, standing 24 m (79 ft) high. Much of the stained glass, probably by Flemish master glaziers, arrived later at the behest of Henry VIII, who had himself depicted as the wise King Solomon in one window. It's the second on the right beyond the oak screen that separates the nave from the choir – another of Henry's additions of the early 1530s, the Italianate work bears his 'H' monogram intertwined with an 'A' for his ill-fated wife, Anne Boleyn. The altarpiece – *Adoration of the Magi* – is by Rubens. A museum, accessed off the choir, relates the chapel's development.

ⓐ King's Parade (entrance Trinity Lane) ☎ 01223 331100
ⓦ www.kings.cam.ac.uk 🕐 09.30–15.30 Mon–Fri, 09.30–15.15 Sat, 13.15–14.30 Sun (in term time); 09.30–16.00 Mon–Sat, 10.00–16.00 Sun (out of term; half-hour later closing in British Summer Time) ❶ Admission charge

Magdalene Bridge & Magdalene College

Bridge Street, the former medieval thoroughfare into Cambridge, sweeps up to Magdalene Bridge (pronounced 'maudlin'), a popular spot to watch the antics of novice punters who embark from a quay beneath. Across the Cam rises Magdalene College. Another Tudor court of red brick and trimmed lawns, it began as a Benedictine hostel for monks and holds the dubious honour of being the last college to admit women, in 1986. Former students include Samuel Pepys, who joined in 1650 – college records reveal his being ticked off by tutors for 'having bene scandalously overseene in drink' one night. The celebrated diarist bequeathed his library to the college in 1703 on condition that it remain intact. So it does in a library in the Second Court, its 3,000 tomes stored in glazed bookcases that Pepys commissioned from dockyard joiners (he was once employed as clerk to the royal docks). The famous diaries are in the first of these, on the back row of the second shelf. ❸ Magdalene Street ☎ 01223 332100 ⓦ www.magd.cam.ac.uk ⓛ College: 09.00–18.00 daily. Pepys Library: see website for details as times vary

🔺 *Magdalene Bridge marks the northern end of the college quarter*

Queens' College

Founded in 1448 by Queen Margaret of Anjou then again by Queen Elizabeth Woodville in 1475 (hence the plural apostrophe), Queens' is arguably the most enchanting college in Cambridge. Its two intimate courtyards are a cocoon of Tudor red brick and half-timbering that preserve the self-contained world of a medieval college: a gatehouse to protect students, accommodation, a kitchen and dining hall, a library and a chapel. The Old Hall that connects the two is contemporary but received a Victorian makeover in the Arts and Crafts style. Alongside portraits of founders inside is one of Desiderius Erasmus, the Flemish religious reformer who lodged at Queens' from 1510. Not that he was fond of Cambridge: the plague and thieves were ubiquitous, he moaned, and the wine and beer terrible. Latter-day Queens' man Stephen Fry has warmer

🔵 *The 'Mathematical Bridge' joins the two halves of Queens' College*

memories of the old place. The oak bridge behind the college is known to everyone as the 'Mathematical Bridge' due to a popular myth that it was a self-supporting structure until dismantled by students to investigate its construction. In fact, the original was built with bolts in 1751, and by a master carpenter not Isaac Newton. ⓐ Queens' Lane ☎ 01223 335537 ⓦ www.queens.cam.ac.uk ⏱ 10.00–16.30 daily (mid-Mar–mid-May & mid-June–Sept); 14.00–16.00 Mon–Fri, 10.00–16.30 Sat & Sun (Oct); 14.00–16.00 daily (Nov–mid-Mar), closed mid-May–mid-June ⓘ Admission charge mid-Mar–Sept

Round Church

Officially the Church of the Holy Sepulchre, this is known to everyone as the Round Church because of its shape. The curio, one of only five of its kind in England, was built in 1130 as a copy of the Holy Sepulchre in Jerusalem. It's worth going inside to soak up the intimacy of the Norman space – a tight circle with an arcade ringed by carved faces – although the effect was altered by a medieval extension. Also within is a permanent exhibition on British Christianity and a video of Cambridge history. ⓐ Bridge Street ☎ 01223 311602 ⓦ www.christianheritage.org.uk ⏱ 10.00–17.00 Tues–Sat, 13.00–17.00 Sun, closed Monday ⓘ Donation requested

St John's College

St John's opens with a Tudor gatehouse with a statue and gilded crest of its 16th-century founder, Lady Margaret Beaufort, mother of Henry VII. The fabulous beasts that support the crest are known as yales, a Tudor flight of fancy cobbled together from the head of a goat, the body of an antelope and the tail of an elephant. Dorothy Wordsworth confessed herself 'awestruck' by the sight when she visited her fresher brother William in 1787. He bunked down in 'a nook obscure' in First Court, the 16th-century red-brick quadrant within the gate – 'gloomy but beautiful', Dorothy observed. The two other courts are contemporary, so the college's celebrated Bridge of Sighs across the Cam to the Backs is a relative newcomer. So-called because it is covered like its Venetian namesake, the neo-Gothic bridge (1831) is, as Queen Victoria pointed out, the most 'pretty and picturesque' part of the college. ❸ St John's Street ❶ 01223 338600 ⓦ www.joh.cam.ac.uk ⓛ 10.00–17.00 daily (Mar–Oct), 10.00–15.30 daily (Nov–Mar) ❶ Admission charge

🔺 *The famous Bridge of Sighs in St John's College*

Senate House & Great St Mary's Church

The white 18th-century hall beside King's is the ceremonial heart of Cambridge University – the place where graduates receive degrees. This ceremony gave rise to the tradition of a 'wooden spoon' prize for the lowest score in a competition – the student who scored fewest marks would collect a 1.5-m (5-ft) painted spoon. Senate House is also famous for a battered Austin 7 van that appeared on its roof on 8 June 1958. Years later, 13 engineering students confessed they had hauled the van up overnight in pieces. Before the building of Senate House in the mid-1700s, graduation ceremonies were in Great St Mary's Church opposite. It was rebuilt in the mid-1400s to cope with the growing congregation – King Henry VII himself donated 100 oak beams for the roof. The tower offers the best views over the colleges in Cambridge. Incidentally, the church chime may sound familiar – it was composed in the 1700s by two undergraduates and popularised by Big Ben in London. ⓐ King's Parade ☎ 01223 741716 🕒 Church: 08.30–17.00; Tower: 10.00–17.00 Mon–Sat (30 minutes earlier in winter), 12.00–17.00 Sun ❶ Admission charge for tower

Trinity College

King's is more famous, but Trinity has more superlatives to its name. It has more members than any other Cambridge college – around 700 undergraduates, 430 graduates and 160 fellows – and is widely held to be the town's richest college. An appealing but false tale has it that students could once walk to Oxford without straying from Trinity land. The college has also educated more members of the aristocracy and royalty than any other

Cambridge college – apt considering it was founded in 1546 on land donated by King Henry VIII. His statue stands above the main gate, his sceptre replaced by a chair leg in a time-honoured student prank. Prince Charles is a recent member of royal alumni. In fact, all scored lower grades than other Trinity men: Isaac Newton, six British prime ministers and two Indian ones (Nehru and Rajiv Gandhi); philosophers like Francis Bacon, Bertrand Russell and Ludwig Wittgenstein; and arts greats such

TRINITY TALES

The most celebrated Trinity tradition is for students to race the clock's 24 chimes (12 high, 12 low) around Great Court during the Great Court Run, a distance of 367 m (1,204 ft) in 43 seconds. Once held at midnight after the Matriculation Dinner, the challenge now takes place at noon after too many drunken falls. A race between students Harold Abrahams and Lord Burghley is immortalised in the film *Chariots of Fire* (not filmed at Trinity because the college would not permit a film crew), despite the fact it never took place; Burghley alone managed the feat in 1927. British Olympic runner Sebastian Coe also pulled it off for a charity race in 1988 – sort of. He made it round in 45.52 seconds, crossing the line as the last chime died away. Another popular tale concerns the court's fountain, in which undergraduate Lord Byron is said to have bathed his tame bear. The story that he chose the pet because dogs were prohibited is hotly denied in official college literature.

🔺 *Trinity's Great Court: the largest court of any Cambridge college*

as Dryden, Byron, Tennyson, Thackeray and Vaughan Williams. Trinity is also one the most beautiful of the Cambridge colleges. Steeped in learning and ruled by porters in bowler hats, it is the very image of ancient academia, especially in the late-Gothic Great Court, most of which dates from the early 1600s. Through the Hall at its back is cloistered Nevile's Court, where Newton first calculated the speed of sound, and the beautiful Wren Library. Completed by the architect in 1695, its dark wood shelves hold valuable manuscripts such as early Shakespeare editions, books from Newton's own library and AA Milne's manuscripts of *Winnie-the-Pooh* and *The House at Pooh Corner*.

ⓐ Trinity Street ☎ 01223 338400 ⓦ www.trin.cam.ac.uk
🕐 College: 09.00–16.00 daily. Wren Library: 12.00–14.00 Mon–Fri, 10.30–12.30 Sat, closed Sunday ❶ Admission charge

THE CITY

CULTURE

Cambridge & County Folk Museum

Just across the crossroads above Magdalene College, the 17th-century timber-frame White Horse Inn now houses a cornucopia of objects gathered from the city and Fens area, all themed into rooms such as the Kitchen, Fens and Folklore or Arts. In the Guest Room keep an eye open for a portrait of Thomas Hobson, a wealthy 17th-century stable-owner who hired horses to students – they could choose any steed at all, so long as it was that closest to the stable door. No choice at all, in other words, hence the phrase 'Hobson's choice'. Despite the portrait's mean looks – and its sarcastic poem by Christ's College student John Milton – Hobson was one of Cambridge's greatest benefactors.
ⓐ 2–3 Castle Street ⓣ 01223 355159 ⓦ www.folkmuseum.org.uk
ⓛ 10.30–17.00 Tues–Sat, 14.00–17.00 Sun, closed Mon
ⓘ Admission charge

Kettle's Yard

This is both an enchanting museum and gallery space. The former was the home of Jim Ede, a curator at the Tate Gallery in London during the 1920s and '30s, whose friendships with artists led him to acquire a remarkable collection of art: paintings by the likes of Ben and Winifred Nicholson, Christopher Wood, David Jones and Joan Miró, as well as sculpture by Henry Moore and Barbara Hepworth. Most works remain in the cottage's rooms, which still house the Edes' furniture to create a museum as charming as it is erudite. The modern gallery space hangs changing exhibitions of 20th-century art and the centre also runs creative kids' workshops several times a month – parents take note. ⓐ Castle Street ⓣ 01223 748100 ⓦ www.kettlesyard.co.uk ⓛ House: 14.00–16.00 Tues–Sun, closed Mon (half-hour earlier & later Apr–Sept). Gallery: 11.30–17.00 Tues–Sun, closed Mon

RETAIL THERAPY

All Saints Art & Craft Market

The triangular garden opposite Trinity College hosts a weekly gathering of independent artisans: expect everything from painting to pottery, ceramics to sculpture, via jewellery, photography and textiles. ⓐ Trinity Street ⓦ www.cambridge-art-craft.co.uk ⓛ Sat (year-round), plus Fri (June–Aug) & Wed–Fri (Dec–Christmas)

Cambridge Cheese Company

Hidden off St John's Street, this foodie delight stocks farmhouse and artisan cheeses and olives, plus local honey and pork pies. Hot soups and sandwiches are available to take away and the shop will rustle up a picnic hamper on request. ⓐ 4 All Saints Passage ⓣ 01223 328672 ⓦ www.cambridgecheese.com ⓛ 10.00–18.00 Mon–Fri, 09.00–17.00 Sat, closed Sun & bank holidays

Cambridge University Press

Affiliated to the university since 1532, the world's oldest bookseller is an academic bookshop par excellence, its shelves are crammed with esoteric texts but still with room for general scholarly works, and books on local architecture and sights. ⓐ 1 Trinity Street ☎ 01223 333333 ⓦ www.cambridge.org/bookshop 🕐 09.00–17.30 Mon–Sat, 11.00–17.00 Sun

Primavera

A tiny crafts shop full of fine things. Whether sculpture, ceramics, glassware, painting or jewellery, all pieces are British and handmade one-offs. ⓐ 10 King's Parade ☎ 01223 357708 ⓦ www.primaverauk.com 🕐 10.00–17.30 Mon–Sat, 11.00–17.00 Sun & bank holidays

Ryder & Amies

Opposite King's, this family-owned outfitter has supplied college clothing for over a century: from ties and scarves in college colours or classic cricket jumpers, to branded sweatshirts and T-shirts. Also stocks kids' clothing and general university souvenirs. ⓐ 22 King's Parade ☎ 01223 350371 ⓦ www.ryderamies.co.uk 🕐 08.30–17.30 Mon–Sat, 10.00–17.00 Sun

TAKING A BREAK

Michaelhouse Café £ ❶ Part community centre, part bohemian student hangout, this arty modern café in the medieval church of St Michael is an excellent stop for coffee or homemade mains prepared daily from local ingredients. ⓐ Trinity Street ☎ 01223 309147 ⓦ www.michaelhousecafe.co.uk 🕐 08.00–17.00 Mon–Sat, closed Sun

Cambridge Chop House ££ ❷ British cuisine is given a contemporary twist in a relaxed bistro-style restaurant: expect the likes of speciality bangers and mash, thick-cut bacon and duck eggs or woodpigeon, pear and hazelnut salad – and, of course, chops. A smarter sister restaurant is on Northampton Street.
ⓐ 2 King's Parade ⓣ 01223 359506 ⓦ www.chophouses.co.uk
ⓛ 12.00–22.30 Mon–Thur, 12.00–23.00 Fri & Sat, 12.00–21.30 Sun

Rainbow Café ££ ❸ A loud, friendly basement restaurant whose vegetarian cuisine, much of it gluten- and nut-free, is acclaimed by students and gourmets alike. Adventurous global dishes complement the usual chillies, pastas and risottos, all of it good value at around £9 a main. Good desserts too. ⓐ 9A King's Parade ⓣ 01223 321551 ⓦ www.rainbowcafe.co.uk ⓛ 10.00–22.00 Tues–Sat, 10.00–16.00 Sun & Mon

AFTER DARK

The Anchor ❹ It's touristy, but the riverside location beside Queens' make The Anchor worth a visit nonetheless, if only for a terrace that offers a grandstand view of the punts in summer.
ⓐ 12 Silver Street ⓣ 01223 353554 ⓛ 10.00–23.00 Mon–Thur, 10.00–24.00 Fri & Sat, 11.00–22.30 Sun

The Pickerel ❺ The sole survivor of five medieval inns by the city gate is a cosy bolthole of low beams and creaky floorboards. Real ales are on tap and there's a rear courtyard for alfresco drinking. ⓐ 30 Magdalene Street ⓣ 01223 355068 ⓛ 12.00–24.00 Tues–Sat, 12.00-23.00 Sun & Mon

The commercial centre

Town replaces gown east of the college quarter. Though not totally bereft of colleges nor of history, Cambridge's core is characterised by high-street shopping. Largely pedestrianised, this is home to the daily market, to busy stores and showpiece modern malls like Grand Arcade. Even those few colleges sited here are of a more commercial bent, largely because their locations make them attractive propositions for summer schools and conferences. Colleges aside, this is a modern area whose looks belie an older heritage. You'd never know, for example, that today's bland 1960s mall Petty Cury was named after its inns and bakeries – 'petit cury' (literally, 'little cooks' row'). Nor is it all window displays; academia reasserts itself to the south of the area through a clutch of university museums and the superb Fitzwilliam.

SIGHTS & ATTRACTIONS

Christ's College

The gilded Great Gate of Christ's, bearing the coat of arms of founder Lady Margaret Beaufort, Henry VII's mother, adds a touch of history to the Lion Yard shopping arcade opposite. It's an appropriate introduction to a college that dates from the mid-1400s. The newer Second Court provides access to Fellows' Garden – Christ's graduate John Milton is dubiously said to have found inspiration for *Paradise Lost* under its mulberry tree. Another Christ's man was Charles Darwin; not a particularly brilliant scholar by all accounts – he devoted more time to collecting beetles than study – but a personable one, which is why in 1831 a 22-year-old bound for the clergy found himself sailing into history instead as a 'gentleman's companion' for the captain of HMS *Beagle*. **ⓐ** St Andrew's Street **ⓣ** 01223 334900 **ⓦ** www.christs.cam.ac.uk **ⓛ** 09.30–16.30 daily (term time); 09.30–12.00 daily (out of term)

Emmanuel College

Emmanuel's sober façade hides a charming arcaded courtyard backed by a Baroque chapel by Christopher Wren. It was the great architect's second Cambridge commission, designed in 1666. Inside is a plaque and stained glass to commemorate John Harvard, a former student who bequeathed a small American college his library of 400 books and £779. It returned the favour and became Harvard University. Harvard was one of around 30 Emmanuel graduates to sail to New England during a crackdown on the college's Calvinist leanings in the 1630s. This also explains why Harvard is in Cambridge, Massachusetts – until the Emmanuel scholars arrived, the settlement was plain old 'Newtown'. **ⓐ** St Andrew's Street **ⓣ** 01223 334200 **ⓦ** www.emma.cam.ac.uk **ⓛ** Daylight hours

Jesus College

Few visitors make it to 'Jesus', the college of literary bad boy Samuel Taylor Coleridge, broadcaster Alistair Cook and HRH Prince Edward, yet its hushed red-brick courts draped in ivy and wisteria are some of the city's loveliest. You approach via 'The Chimney', actually a 'lane' (from the French chemin), then duck through a gatehouse to enter a college laid out over an early medieval Benedictine nunnery; the Bishop of Ely established Jesus in 1496 after the nunnery's dissolution. You can sense the ecclesiastical past in intimate Cloister Court, on the right beyond the gatehouse, while the chapel off it retains the fabric of the early 13th-century nunnery church, making it the oldest college building in Cambridge. Its stained glass in the choir is by pre-Raphaelite artists Sir Edward Burne-Jones, Augustus Pugin and William Morris, who also supplied the roof painting. ⓐ Jesus Lane ⓣ 01223 339339 ⓦ www.jesus.cam.ac.uk ⓒ Daylight hours

🔺 *Jesus College has a number of sculptures scattered about the grounds*

Pembroke College

The chapel that launched the career of architect Christopher Wren is the star turn of this college founded in the 14th century. Designed in 1663, it represented a slice of luck for Wren, then a professor of astronomy at Oxford rather than an architect. The commission was a gift from his uncle, Matthew Wren, then Bishop of Ely, who made good on a vow to fund a chapel for his college while imprisoned in the Tower of London for his Royalist allegiance during the Civil War. The result is this pleasingly austere classical number. ⓐ Trumpington Street ⓣ 01223 338100 ⓦ www.pem.cam.ac.uk ⓛ Daylight hours

Peterhouse & Little St Mary's Church

Welcome to the first Cambridge college, established by the Bishop of Ely in 1284, and the smallest with 400 students; alumni include Charles Babbage, computer pioneer, jet engine inventor Sir Frank Whittle and comedian David Mitchell. Only the hall remains from the medieval college – its interior is by pre-Raphaelite artists Sir Edward Burne-Jones and William Morris – while the rather flamboyant chapel dates from the 1632. Earlier students used the attached gothic church, Little St Mary's, whose former name St Peter's christened the college. A tablet inside remembers a former vicar, Godfrey Washington, the great-uncle of the American president. The stars, stripes and eagle of the family arms were adapted to create the American flag in 1776. ⓐ Trumpington Street ⓣ 01223 338200 ⓦ www.pet.cam.ac.uk ⓛ Daylight hours

St Bene't's Church

Hidden around the corner from Market Hill is the oldest
building in Cambridgeshire. The tower of this parish church
was built circa 1020, when King Canute sat on the English
throne, Cambridge was a small town by Magdalene Bridge
and this area was largely a swamp. It's a typically Saxon
construction, from the round holes in its tower to encourage
owls to nest to the splendid round arch inside with mythical
beasts at its base. The nave and choir are medieval. The church's
other claim to fame is as the birthplace of change-ringing
(the sequential pealing of bells of different pitches), instigated
by parish clerk Fabian Stedman in 1663. ⓐ Bene't Street
ⓦ www.stbenetschurch.org

CULTURE

Fitzwilliam Museum

If you only visit one museum in Cambridge, make it this one –
it has exhibits that would not disgrace a capital city. Behind its
massive colonnaded façade is a series of superb collections,
most bequeathed by private benefactors. The ground floors
house antiquities from Rome, Greece and Egypt, notably a
massive, seven-ton sarcophagus lid of Ramesses III, donated by
George Basevi, the architect who created the grandiose building
in the 1840s. There are also ancient Greek and European
ceramics, and applied arts from the Islamic world and Far East –
the museum made the headlines in 2006 when one visitor
tripped over his shoelaces and shattered three 17th-century
Chinese vases. The clear-up alone took nearly three days,

🔺 *The Fitzwilliam Museum is one of the most imposing buildings in Cambridge*

so it's no surprise the restored items are now in a display
case. The first floor has a blockbuster display of European
painting that includes many of the heroes of Italian, French
and British art, the latter extending into the late 20th
century. ❸ Trumpington Street ☎ 01223 332900
🌐 www.fitzmuseum.cam.ac.uk 🕐 10.00–17.00 Tues–Sat,
12.00–17.00 Sun, closed Mon

Museum of Archaeology & Anthropology
The most accessible of the university museums offers a
wonderland of anthropological curios to browse. On the ground
floor are archaeological finds, from the earliest hominid tools
from Africa to Roman and medieval objects unearthed in the
Cambridge area. The upper gallery is devoted to ethnography –
the museum is worth a visit for the enormous native American
totem pole alone – including objects acquired by Captain
James Cook on his voyage into the South Pacific. Note that a
modernisation programme until late 2011 may close some
sections of the museum. ❸ Downing Street ☎ 01223 333516
🌐 www.maa.cam.ac.uk 🕐 10.30–16.30 Tues–Sat, closed
Sun & Mon

Sedgwick Museum of Earth Sciences
A counterpart to the zoology museum is this hoard of animal
and plant fossils gathered from around the world. A number of
the dinosaur skeletons will wow young children – the most
impressive is that of the Iguanodon that forms the museum
centrepiece – and there are sections on the formation of the
planet and its geology. Incidentally, the museum is named after

Adam Sedgwick, a college scientist who taught geology to Charles Darwin. Later, Darwin posted a copy of *On the Origin of Species* to his mentor. 'I have read your book with more pain than pleasure,' Sedgwick replied. 'Parts of it I admired greatly; parts I laughed at till my sides were almost sore.' ⓐ Downing Street ⓣ 01223 333456 ⓦ www.sedgwickmuseum.org ⓛ 10.00–13.00 & 14.00–17.00 Mon–Fri, 10.00–16.00 Sat, closed Sun

University Museum of Zoology

At least one specimen of every group of animal, both fossil and living, is on display in the extensive collection of the university's nature museum. With that evolutionary angle, it's no surprise the museum's star turn is an exhibition of specimens collected by Christ's College graduate Charles Darwin during his five-year expedition aboard HMS *Beagle*. These include some of the famous Galapagos finches with which Darwin supported *On the Origin of Species*, published in 1859. Special events are held throughout the year. ⓐ Downing Street ⓣ 01223 336650 ⓦ www.museum.zoo.cam.ac.uk ⓛ 10.00–16.45 Mon–Fri, 11.00–16.00 Sat, closed Sun ⓝ Bus: City Circle

RETAIL

Cambridge Toy Shop Catering to ages up to around 14, the city's premier toy outlet is just the ticket to keep the little ones quiet, with a wide selection of toys, puzzles, crafts and cute furry things. An antidote to the usual bland chains. ⓐ 15–16 Sussex Street ⓣ 01223 309010 ⓛ 09.30–17.30 Mon–Sat, 11.00–17.00 Sun

Chocolat Chocolat All manner of handmade French-inspired treats, including trademark chocolate sheets with nuts and berries. A rich hot chocolate prepared in winter is a splendidly decadent way to beat the chill. **ⓐ** 21 St Andrew's Street **ⓣ** 01223 778982 **ⓛ** 09.00–18.00 Mon–Tues & Thur–Fri, 09.00–20.00 Wed, 09.00–19.00 Sat, 10.30–18.00 Sun

The Haunted Bookshop This tiny place on a side lane is the second-hand bookshop par excellence. It specialises in out-of-print children's books and first editions. **ⓐ** 9 St Edward's Passage **ⓣ** 01223 312913 **ⓛ** 10.00–17.00 Mon–Sat, closed Sun & bank holidays

▲ *Petty Cury is a compact but busy shopping street*

TAKE A BREAK

Clowns £ 6 A charming and cheerfully decorated café situated close to, but not on, the tourist trail. Run by a friendly Italian family, this makes an excellent spot for grabbing a cup of coffee and a bite to eat. Their pasta dishes come especially recommended. **a** 54 King Street **t** 01223 355711 **c** 08.00–22.45 daily

Trockel, Ulmann & Freunde £ 7 A simple lively café that provides a pitstop between museums – filled baguettes and interesting homemade soups are on the menu. **a** 13 Pembroke Street **t** 09.00–17.00 Mon–Fri, 10.00–17.00 Sat, closed Sun

Charlie Chan's ££ 8 Fresh high-quality ingredients and careful preparation go into the finest Chinese food in the region, with all the classic dishes such as crispy Peking duck plus excellent lunchtime dim sum. There's live dinner jazz downstairs at weekends. **a** 14 Regent Street **t** 01223 359336 **c** 12.00–23.00 daily

Fitzbillies ££ 9 Acclaimed for the sticky Chelsea buns sold in an attached bakers since 1922, this famous café-restaurant has raised its game with a dinner menu (Fri–Sat only) of British and Mediterranean cuisine. **a** 52 Trumpington Street **t** 01223 352500 **w** www.fitzbillies.co.uk **c** 09.30–17.30 Mon, 09.30–22.00 Tues–Sun

Jamie's Italian ££ 10 That's 'Jamie's' as in TV chef Jamie Oliver, so you can expect excellent Italian cuisine and a lively atmosphere in its two dining rooms – a bistro-style front room and rear atrium created in the old town library. ⓐ The Old Library, Wheeler Street ⓣ 01223 654094 ⓦ www.jamieoliver.com/Italian ⓛ 12.00–23.00 Mon–Sat, 12.00–22.30 Sun

AFTER DARK

Arts Picturehouse ⓫ Small repertory cinema that screens arthouse films, plus more interesting Hollywood releases. ⓐ 38–39 St Andrew's Street ⓣ 0871 704 2050 ⓦ www.picturehouses.co.uk

Cambridge Arts Theatre ⓬ The premier stage in Cambridge – paid for by economist John Maynard Keynes – programmes a repertoire of everything from musicals to modern plays via Shakespeare and classics. As former home of the student Footlights Revue, it has acted as a springboard for many greats of British comedy. ⓐ 6 St Edward's Passage (between King's Parade & Peas Hill) ⓣ 01223 503333 ⓦ www.cambridgeartstheatre.com

Cambridge Corn Exchange ⓭ The former trading hall for local farmers is now the principal venue for a diverse range of entertainment: concerts of classical music and crowd-pleasers, dance, musicals, touring rock bands and occasional comedy gigs. ⓐ Wheeler Street ⓣ 01223 357581 ⓦ www.cornex.co.uk

Champion of the Thames ⓮ Lovely side-street pub, a bolthole of warm old wood, low ceilings and community spirit that's an antidote to the bland pubs in the centre. Good Greene King and guests ales on draught. ⓐ 68 King Street ⓣ 01223 352043 ⓛ 12.00–23.00 Mon–Thur & Sun, 11.00–23.00 Fri & Sat

The Eagle ⓯ A coaching inn from the 1600s, the Eagle has seen plenty of history: World War II airmen drank – and wrote a signature in soot on the roof – in the RAF bar, and Francis Crick and James Watson announced their discovery of DNA in the bar. Touristy in season, The Eagle has been refurbished in recent years and is well worth a visit. ⓐ 8 Bene't Street ⓣ 01223 505020 ⓛ 10.00–23.00 Mon–Sat, 10.00–22.30 Sun

Fez ⓰ With parties seven days a week during term time and occasional superstar DJ sets, this snug venue provides the best clubbing in the centre; expect nights of house, indie, hip hop, funk and R'n'B. Monday night is student night. ⓐ 15 Market Passage ⓣ 01223 519224 ⓦ www.cambridgefez.com ⓛ 22.00–03.00 daily

● *Market Square is a great place for finding food, gifts and much else besides*

Beyond the centre

Beyond its centre, Cambridge lapses into a series of residential neighbourhoods that appeared as the city boomed in the 1800s. Aside from revealing a slice of real life outside the academic bubble of the centre, these neighbourhoods are interspersed by some magnificent green spaces – arguably Cambridge's trump card over its great rival Oxford. Factor in a fine, vast and picturesque botanic garden and more scenic paths along the river, and this area offers a balance to the history of the centre.

SIGHTS & ATTRACTIONS

Botanic Garden

Over 8,000 plants in 16 landscaped hectares (40 acres) provide a whistle-stop tour of global flora just ten minutes' walk south of the Fitzwilliam Museum (see pages 64–6). Opened in 1831 by Professor John Stevens Henslow, Charles Darwin's botany professor, the university-affiliated gardens are noted for their scientific value; they hold ten National Collections of plant species and several of the large greenhouses investigate plant evolution – children are sure to love the carnivorous plants – while the opening of the Sainsbury Laboratory at the end of 2010 added world-class research facilities. Yet the main reason to visit remains the idyllic vistas and a masterclass in planting.

ⓐ Entry Trumpington Road & Hills Road–Station Road junction ⓘ 01223 336265 ⓛ 10.00–18.00 daily (Apr–Sept); 10.00–17.00 daily (Feb, Mar & Oct); 10.00–16.00 daily (Nov & Jan) ⓝ Bus: Uni 4 ⓘ Admission charge

Jesus Green & Midsummer Common

This pleasant park lies wedged between the river and Jesus College – it's a lovely walk from Magdalene Bridge along the river. En route, screened by trees, lies the longest lido in the country, a 100-m (328-ft) pool of 1920s vintage. Across Victoria Avenue is Midsummer Common, site of town fairs since Elizabethan days. Continue on the riverside path and you'll pass college boathouses on the opposite bank. During term time, expect to see crews training for the intercollegiate 'May Bumps' rowing races – held in June, naturally. Lido ⓐ Jesus Green ① 01223 302579 ① 12.00–19.30 (from 10.30 school holidays) Mon, Wed & Thur, 07.30–19.30 Tues & Fri 11.00–19.30 Sat & Sun (May–Sept) ① Admission charge

🔺 *Jesus Green is a popular picnicking spot on sunny days*

Parker's Piece & Mill Road

Welcome to the birthplace of football. The first match played under students' Cambridge Rules – no more catching the ball, no more 'hacking' of ankles – was played on this park east of the centre in 1848, and the rules were enshrined in the Association Football rules. The park is known locally for its lonely central lamp post dubbed 'Reality Checkpoint', possibly because it represents the unofficial boundary between academia and the 'real world' beyond. The latter is Mill Road, on the far side of the park. Long a bastion of student accommodation, it is one of the most cosmopolitan central neighbourhoods in Cambridge, with a clutch of international cafés, foreign-food supermarkets, a bookshop or two and some excellent pubs – student heaven.
ⓐ St Andrew's Street/Parkside ⓝ Bus: Citi 2

CULTURE

Museum of Technology

Continue along the river from Midsummer Common to reach this Victorian pumping station. Its massive two-cylinder steam engines – the last of their kind operational in the world – were installed to tackle a crisis during the city's rapid expansion in the late 1800s, when sewage was flushed directly into the Cam. As the Master of Trinity College said dryly when Queen Victoria inquired about squares of paper floating in the river: 'Those, Ma'am, are notices prohibiting bathing.' The station also includes vintage gas and electric pumps in its narrative of industrial technology development. ⓐ The Old Pumping Station, Cheddar's Lane (off Riverside) ⓣ 01223 368650

🌐 www.museumoftechnology.com 🕐 14.00–17.00 every Sun (Easter–Oct), 1st Sun in month (Nov–Easter), closed Mon–Sat 🚍 Bus: Citi 3 ❶ Admission charge

Scott Polar Research Institute & Museum

Renovation in 2010 has rejuvenated this small museum that displays the institute's polar memorabilia. Manuscripts, watercolours, prints, drawings and photos are arranged in thematic displays such as travel, native people, wildlife or scientific research. Yet it's the exhibits devoted to the 'heroes' of Antarctic exploration in the early 1900s that really seize the imagination: Ernest Shackleton's chronometer or evacuation instructions stained by fat from the blubber stove, or, most poignantly, the final letters and diaries written by Captain Scott and his party to mothers and wives. 📍 Lensfield Road ☎ 01223 336540 🌐 www.spri.cam.ac.uk 🕐 10.00–16.00 Tues–Sun, closed Mon 🚍 Bus: Citi 4

TAKE A BREAK

Oak Bistro ££ ⓱ Consistently tasty modern European dishes such as goat's cheese with fig marmalade or duck confit are served in this stylish modern bistro-restaurant near Parker's Piece and the polar museum. Set lunch menus offer excellent value and there's a lovely courtyard for summer dining. 📍 6 Lensfield Road ☎ 01223 323361 🌐 www.theoakbistro.co.uk 🕐 12.00–24.00 Mon–Fri, 11.00–24.00 Sat, closed Sun

Midsummer House £££ ⓰ This Victorian villa remains the destination for a splurge thanks to the creative Michelin-starred

cuisine of its master-chef, Daniel Clifford, with a taste for modern British and French. No Michelin food snobbery here, though – a conservatory dining room with just 12 tables and friendly staff make for an intimate atmosphere. ⓐ Midsummer Common (by footbridge) ⓣ 01223 369299 `
ⓦ www.midsummerhouse.co.uk ⓛ 12.00–13.45 & 19.00–21.30 Wed–Sat, 19.00–21.30 Tues, closed Sun & Mon

Restaurant 22 £££ ⓳ Excellent classic French and English dishes in a converted house across the Cam from Jesus Green. Expect

⬤ Boathouses and narrow boats line the river at Midsummer Common

the likes of whelk fritters with shaved fennel and sour cream or roast belly of pork with boulangère potatoes, broccoli and chorizo oil. ❸ 22 Chesterton Road ☎ 01223 351880 🌐 www.restaurant22.co.uk 🕐 19.00–21.45 Tues–Sat, closed Sun & Mon

AFTER DARK

Cambridge Blue ⓴ Arguably the best of several fine pubs off Mill Road, this friendly place with boat race memorabilia benefits from a community atmosphere and top-notch real ales – an ideal pub to while away a wet afternoon or a sunny evening in the beer garden. ❸ 85–87 Gwydir Street ☎ 01223 361382 🌐 www.the-cambridgeblue.co.uk 🕐 12.00–23.00 Mon–Sat, 12.00–22.30 Sun

Fort St George ㉑ Ten minutes' walk along the river from Magdalene Bridge is this 16th-century inn, a slice of country living in the city whose riverside location is a lovely spot to while away summer. ❸ Midsummer Common ☎ 01223 354327 🕐 11.00–23.00 Mon–Thur, 11.00–24.00 Fri & Sat, 11.00–22.30 Sun

Free Press ㉒ Hidden on a backstreet north of Parker's Piece, this tiny pub is as local as it gets; just three rooms, an older academic clientele, and excellent fresh ales and food. No flashy fittings, no fruit machines, no mobile phones and no muzak – all in all, a gem. ❸ 7 Prospect Row ☎ 01223 368337 🌐 www.freepresspub.com 🕐 12.00–14.30 & 18.00–23.00 Mon–Fri, 12.00–23.00 Sat, 12.00–15.00 & 19.00–22.30 Sun

The Granta ㉓ Often besieged by tourists, the balcony and terrace overlooking willow-fringed millponds make this otherwise simple pub essential. If you feel inspired, there's punt hire beside the pub. ⓐ 14 Newnham Road ⓣ 01223 505016 ⓛ 11.00–23.00 Sun–Thur, 11.00–24.00 Fri & Sat

The Junction ㉔ Near the junction of Hills and Cherry Hinton roads, this multi-venue centre is the wellspring of cool Cambridge; there are hip gigs, contemporary dance and theatre, comedy from touring acts and cutting-edge club nights. ⓐ Clifton Way ⓣ 01223 511511 ⓦ www.junction.co.uk ⓝ Bus: Citi 3

Vue Cinema ㉕ Mainstream releases in an eight-screen multiplex in the Grafton Centre, between Midsummer Common and Parker's Piece. ⓐ Grafton Centre ⓣ 01223 213352 ⓦ www.myvue.com

West Road Concert Hall ㉖ Excellent acoustics and a policy to programme around four concerts a week make the university concert hall behind the Backs, home to three resident ensembles, one of the city's premier stages for classical music. ⓐ 11 West Road ⓣ 01223 335184 ⓦ www.westroad.org ⓝ Bus: Citi 4

● *For something a little different, head to the Imperial War Museum at Duxford*

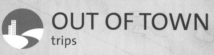

OUT OF TOWN
trips

To the south

Cambridge dominates the region but several sights nearby make ideal daytrips. From a stately home to super-fighters, there is something here for all the family.

Grantchester

'Stands the clock at ten to three/And is there honey still for tea?' Rupert Brooke wondered in his poem to 'the lovely hamlet Grantchester'. From 1909–14, the war poet lived in the idyllic village 5 km (3 miles) southwest of Cambridge as a King's student, travelling downriver to lectures by canoe. Many visitors now make the same trip in reverse by punting up or walking on a riverside path from Cambridge. Brooke's story is told in a museum in the **Orchard Tea Garden**, where the poet had cream teas with his undergraduate friends: EM Forster, Virginia Woolf, Bertrand Russell, Ludwig Wittgenstein and John Maynard Keynes. This is a blissful setting that has barely changed in a century. ⓐ 45 Mill Way ⓣ 01223 845788 ⓦ www.orchard-grantchester.com ⓛ 09.30–16.30 daily (Dec–Feb); 09.30–17.30 daily (Mar–May & Sept–Nov); 09.30–19.00 daily (June–Aug) Ⓝ Bus: 18

Imperial War Museum Duxford

Many airfields were established throughout Cambridgeshire during World War II. Duxford, 15 km (9 miles) south of Cambridge, played a front-line role in the Battle of Britain – fighter ace Douglas Bader's Squadron 242 was stationed here – then acted as a base for American airmen. Now it houses what aficionados rank as the finest air museum in Europe. Its hangars

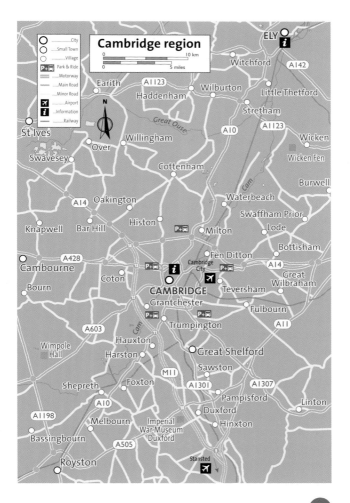

hold the largest collection of historic aircraft on the continent – from vintage biplanes to space-age jets. You can also see the original 1940s Operation Room, aircraft restorers at work, and displays of land and sea warfare. Duxford hosts four or five outstanding air shows a year and operates pleasure flights (May–October ⓦ www.classic-wings.co.uk). ⓐ Junction 10, M11 ⓣ 01223 835000 ⓦ www.iwm.org.uk/duxford ⓛ 10.00–18.00 daily (mid-Mar–late Oct); 10.00–16.00 daily (Nov–mid-Mar) Ⓝ Bus: Citi 7 (Mon–Sat), Myalls 132 (Sun) ⓘ Admission charge

Wimpole Hall

This National Trust-owned 1,000-hectare (2,500-acre) estate is one for all the family. At its centre, 13 km (8 miles) southwest of Cambridge, is the region's largest country house, built in 1643, then tinkered with by future landowners – one added two wings solely for a visit by Queen Victoria. The finest interiors are by Georgian architect Sir John Soane, while the furnishings were gathered by the last owner, Elsie Bambridge, daughter of Rudyard Kipling, who made it her life's work to reassemble the original fittings. The Hall's history is as much about its gardens as the house. Great landscapers such as Capability Brown played a role in creating its avenues and serpentine lakes. A ten-minute walk through the Pleasure Grounds brings you to the children's favourite, Wimpole Home Farm, a late 18th-century working farmstead. ⓐ Arrington, Royston ⓣ 01223 206000 ⓦ www.wimpole.org ⓛ Hall: 10.30–17.00 Sat–Wed (Apr–Oct), closed Thur & Fri (except late July & Aug when Thur open). Gardens: 10.30–17.00 daily (Apr–Oct); 11.00–16.00 Sat–Wed, closed Thur–Fri (Nov–Mar). Farm: 10.30–17.00 daily (Apr–Oct);

11.00–16.00 Sat & Sun, closed Mon–Wed (Nov–Mar) 🔄 Bus: 75 from Cambridge, then 1.5 km (1 mile) walk from bus stop at Arrington. Return from Orwell, 2.4 km (1½ miles) away; seek directions in visitor centre ❶ Admission charge

TAKE A BREAK

Green Man ££ Rough cob walls, battered leather armchairs, log fires and real ales on draught – this central pub near the village church is a slice of rural England. There's above-average pub food on the menu and a beer garden. ⓐ 59 High Street, Grantchester ☎ 01223 844669

John Barleycorn ££ Airmen of the Duxford Wing supped in this smart 17th-century coaching inn in Duxford village, serving excellent cask ales and a good-value British menu. ⓐ 3 Moorfield Road, Duxford ☎ 01223 832699

🔺 *Wimpole Hall makes a great day out for all the family*

To the north

ELY

With its Georgian houses, sleepy riverfront and teashops, Ely is a place to potter after the buzz of Cambridge. Yet the small Fenland town was the regional power while much of present-day Cambridge was swamp. The reason is the **cathedral** that dominates the skyline: 'the Ship of the Fens', once elevated above marshland on a low island. Add in the excellent nature reserve en route if you have your own transport.

Three trains an hour go direct from Cambridge to Ely; the journey takes 15 minutes. Turn left from the station and walk for ten minutes up Back Hill to reach the cathedral.

Ely Cathedral

An abbey was established here as early as AD 673, but it took a century of ferrying stone and oak to complete today's Norman building in 1189. The collapse of the square tower in 1322 led architects to push back the foundations in search of firmer ground to create the unique octagon at the crossing. Its masterpiece of medieval mathematics – a 400-tonne lattice of lead and oak that resolved the problem of supporting the wider tower – can be seen on a tour. Other highlights include a beautiful Romanesque nave, and the choir whose aisles contain tombs of past bishops, including what may be the shrine to abbey founder St Ethelreda. Don't miss the high Gothic Lady Chapel off the north aisle. The largest cathedral chapel in Britain leaves you in no doubt about the violent iconoclasm of the Reformation: every saint is beheaded. ❸ The Gallery, Ely

① 01353 667735 ⓦ www.elycathedral.org ⓒ 07.00–19.00 daily (summer); 07.30–18.00 Mon–Sat, 07.30–17.00 Sun (winter) ① Admission charge

Riverside

Five minutes' walk through the park behind the cathedral or down the high street brings you to the **River Ouse**. Canal boats and the *Liberty Belle* pleasure cruiser (ⓐ Waterside ① 01353 777567 ⓒ 12.00–16.30 Sat–Thur, closed Fri (May–Sept)) now moor to the quay from which grain and heavy machinery were loaded, while a former barn at the wharf houses an antiques centre (see page 88).

The **Cawdle Fen Walk** takes three to four hours to loop 10 km (6 miles) through fen waterways while the flat 27-km (17-mile) **Fens Rivers Way** follows the river back to Cambridge. Leaflets with maps on both walks are available in Ely visitor centre in Oliver Cromwell's House (see page 86).

⬤ *Ely Cathedral: 'Ship of the Fens'*

Wicken Fen

The National Trust's Wicken Fen, midway between Cambridge and Ely, preserves a unique remnant of the ancient wetlands that blanketed the region for centuries until the Fens were drained in the 1600s. A refuge for Boudicca's Iceni and Saxon rebel Hereward the Wake, its maze of waterways and reedbeds now protect the diverse flora and fauna; the 8,000-odd species here make the fen the most biodiverse place in Britain. You may see an astonishing variety of waterbirds and birds of prey such as hen-harriers or hear the booming call of bitterns on a 1.2-km (3/4-mile) boardwalk. The two-mile Nature Trail and Adventurers' Trail pass through grasslands where herds of highland cattle and ghost-grey konik ponies graze. There are also options for boat trips in summer.
ⓐ Lode Lane, Wicken (A1123 off A10) ❶ 01353 720274
ⓦ www.wicken.org.uk ❶ 10.00–17.00 daily ❶ Admission charge

CULTURE

Oliver Cromwell's House

Until he routed Charles II's army in 1647 on the way to becoming Lord Protector of England, Oliver Cromwell lived with his family in this timber-frame house as Ely's tax collector. Rooms of the listed building have been furnished to suggest the early life of the United Kingdom's only republican leader. Apparently some visitors report feeling his ghost in his former study and bedroom. ⓐ 29 St Mary's Street ❶ 01353 662062
ⓦ www.olivercromwellshouse.co.uk ❶ 10.00–17.00 daily (Apr–Oct); 11.00–16.00 Mon–Thur & 10.00–17.00 Fri–Sun (Nov–Mar)
❶ Admission charge

Stained Glass Museum

The south transept of the country's finest Norman cathedral is
an apt home for its only museum of stained-glass art. Pieces
span nine centuries, from medieval religious works to the
Victorian pieces and modern artwork. ⓐ Ely Cathedral
ⓣ 01353 660347 ⓦ www.stainedglassmuseum.com
ⓛ 10.30–17.00 Mon–Sat, 12.00–18.00 Sun (till 16.30 Nov–Easter)
ⓘ Admission charge

TAKE A BREAK

Peacocks Tearoom £ Pastels and check tableclothes lend a 1930s
country ambience to the Tea Guild's top UK tearoom of 2007.
The setting in a Georgian house on the riverside appeals as
much as the menu: delicious salads, homemade soups and
sandwiches, cakes and scones made fresh each day. Have fun
with the menu of 72 teas. ⓐ 65 Waterside ⓣ 01353 661100
ⓦ www.peacockstearoom.co.uk ⓛ 10.00–17.00 Wed–Sun, closed
Mon & Tues except bank holidays)

Almonry Restaurant & Tea Rooms ££ Sustenance is still provided
to laypeople in the cathedral building where monks donated
alms. As well as lunch in that restaurant – all whitewashed
walls and wooden floors – you can take tea in the gardens
behind the cathedral, the most idyllic spot in Ely on sunny days.
ⓐ 36 High Street ⓣ 01353 666360 ⓛ 09.00–17.00 daily

The Boathouse ££ Fine dining in a relaxed riverside restaurant
whose tasty modern British cuisine is cooked up from local,

seasonal produce. Call ahead to reserve an outdoor table beside the river. ⓐ 5 Annesdale ⓣ 01353 664388 ⓦ www.cambscuisine.com ⓛ 12.00–14.30 & 18.30–21.00 Mon–Thur, 12.00–14.30 & 18.15–21.30 Fri & Sat, 12.00–14.30 & 18.30–20.30 Sun

RETAIL THERAPY

Market Place
Markets come in three flavours in Ely: there's a general market on Thursdays; crafts and collectibles on Saturdays; and a farmers' market every second and fourth Saturday (look out for local smoked eels). ⓐ Market Place

Waterside Antiques
Many Cambridgeshire residents travel to Ely solely for this former barn on Ely wharf, its three floors chock-a-block with antiques and collectibles, as well as good old-fashioned junk garnered from Fenland barns. ⓐ The Wharf ⓣ 01353 667066

◗ *Leave the car at home and discover Cambridge by pedal-power instead*

PRACTICAL
information

Directory

GETTING THERE
By air

The nearest airport is Stansted (**❶** 0844 335 1803
Ⓦ www.stanstedairport.com) – budget air carriers such as
Ryanair (**Ⓦ** www.ryanair.com) and **easyJet** (**Ⓦ** www.easyjet.com)
fly here from 160 destinations.

Many people are aware that air travel emits CO_2, which
contributes to climate change. You may be interested in
the possibility of lessening the environmental impact
of your flight through the charity **Climate Care**
(**Ⓦ** www.jpmorganclimatecare.com), which offsets your CO_2
by funding environmental projects around the world.

By rail

First Capital Connect operates direct rail services between
Cambridge and London King's Cross and **National Express East
Anglia** (NXEA) has direct trains from Liverpool Street.
First Capital Connect **❶** 0845 026 4700
Ⓦ www.firstcapitalconnect.co.uk
National Express East Anglia **❶** 0870 333 4876
Ⓦ www.nationalexpresseastanglia.com
National Rail Enquiries **❶** 0845 748 4950
Ⓦ www.nationalrail.co.uk

By coach

National Express has coaches to Cambridge from cities
throughout the UK. Coming from Scotland and some cities in

the North may require a change at Birmingham or Milton Keynes. Budget coach carrier **Megabus** connects to Oxford. The central terminus for both is on Parkside, beside Parker's Piece.

National Express ☏ 0871 781 8178 Ⓦ www.nationalexpress.com

Megabus ☏ 0871 266 3333 Ⓦ http://megabus.com/uk

By car

Cambridge is at the head of the M11 motorway, around 80 km (50 miles) north of London. Arriving from the North on the A1 and M1, you link to the A14 dual-carriageway, which takes you directly into the city. You also take the A14 to the centre if coming from destinations to the east or west. Be aware that parking in the centre can be difficult – the Park & Ride scheme is worth considering (see page 38).

HEALTH, SAFETY & CRIME

Cambridge is generally a convivial, easygoing sort of place. Although 'town and gown' tension rears its ugly head occasionally, usually as a result of alcohol, and weekend nights in the centre can be boisterous, physical violence is rare. Similarly, the crime rate is low, so visitors are unlikely to feel threatened in the town. That said, take the usual precautions about pickpockets and do not leave valuable possessions unattended in open view in public spaces such as bars and cafés or in your car.

EMERGENCY CONTACTS

If you need to see a doctor or dentist during your visit, either ask your hotel for details of a local practice or phone NHS Direct

(☎ 0845 4647), which gives advice and can direct you to the help you require.

Hospital Addenbrooke's Hospital ❷ Hills Road ☎ 01223 245151 ⓦ www.cuh.org.uk/addenbrookes

OPENING HOURS

Shops 09.00–17.30 Mon–Sat. Larger department stores, tourist-friendly shops and boutiques also open Sun (approx 11.00–17.00).
Banks Generally 09.00–17.00 Mon–Fri, though some in the shopping district also open 10.00–16.00 Sat.

TOILETS

There are public toilets at: Lion Yard arcade, Drummer Street (at bus station), Park Street car park, Quayside (beside Magdalene Bridge), Jesus Green (near the lido), Silver Street (by the bridge) and on Gonville Place (south corner of Parker's Piece). They are generally open from 08.00–20.00 and all are free except those on Park Street and Gonville Place, which cost 20p. All public toilets are accessible to wheelchairs, though some require users to have a Radar key.

CHILDREN

Cambridge is a mixed bag for children. On the one hand, it is compact and friendly, with car-free streets and parks within easy reach. On the other, few indeed are the children that will happily tour historic colleges. The zoology and anthropology museums or that of the Scott Polar Research (see page 75) Institute may appeal to children of a more studious nature, and Kettle's Yard (see pages 56–7) schedules an outstanding arts programme. A number of child-friendly daytrips lie outside in the form of Duxford aviation museum (see pages 80–82), Wimpole Farm (see pages 82–3), with its hands-on children's farm, and the wetland wonderland of Wicken Fen (see page 86).

TRAVELLERS WITH DISABILITIES

There are two main **Shopmobility** centres, both in shopping centres: Grand Arcade Shopmobility (ⓘ 01223 457452) and Grafton Centre Shopmobility in the Grafton Centre East Car Park (ⓘ 01223 461858). Both operate from 10.00–16.00 Mon–Fri. A further office is at the bus station in Drummer Street but the service must be pre-booked (ⓘ 01223 457452). Disabled drivers with a badge are eligible for three hours' discounted parking in central car parks – press the 'Help' button as you enter – and can park in designated bays. They can also park for free in any pay and display space. City Circle buses and most colleges are accessible to wheelchairs.

FURTHER INFORMATION

The Visitor Information Centre is just off Market Square. It stocks leaflets on sights and tours, has flyers for concerts and theatre, sells maps and can book accommodation. 'Love Cambridge', a partnership of central businesses and government, distributes free leaflets on topics such as transport, shopping and eating out.

VisitCambridge Visitor Information Centre ⓐ Wheeler Street ⓘ 0871 226 8006 ⓦ www.visitcambridge.org ⓛ 10.00–17.30 Mon–Fri, 10.00–17.00 Sat, 11.00–15.00 Sun & bank holidays (May–Sept), 10.00–17.00 Mon–Sat, closed Sun (Oct–Apr)

Love Cambridge ⓦ www.love-cambridge.co.uk

ACKNOWLEDGEMENTS

The photographs in this book were taken by Joni Audas and Zenna West for Thomas Cook Publishing, to whom the copyright belongs, except for the following: iStockphoto pages 83 (Peter Bates) & 85 (George Cairns); Shutterstock pages 79 (Paul Drabot) & 55 (David Young).

Project editor: Frances Darby
Copy editor: Ismay Atkins
Proofreaders: Beth Beemer & Emma Haigh
Layout: Julie Crane
Indexer: Penelope Kent

AUTHOR BIOGRAPHY

James Stewart is a travel journalist for national newspapers and magazines, and has written guidebooks for various publishers. He lived in a village near Cambridge for 16 years and began his love affair with the town – and its pubs – as a student at one of its colleges.

Send your thoughts to
books@thomascook.com

- Found a great bar, club, shop or must-see sight that we don't feature?
- Like to tip us off about any information that needs a little updating?
- Want to tell us what you love about this handy little guidebook and more importantly how we can make it even handier?

Then here's your chance to tell all! Send us ideas, discoveries and recommendations today and then look out for your valuable input in the next edition of this title.

Email the above address (stating the title) or write to: pocket guides Series Editor, Thomas Cook Publishing, PO Box 227, Coningsby Road, Peterborough PE3 8SB, UK.